for
MOMS

Just for MOMS

Helping You and Your Daughter on Her Journey to Womanhood

ELIZABETH M. HOEKSTRA
AND M. BETH CUTAIAR

CROSSWAY BOOKS • WHEATON, ILLINOIS
A DIVISION OF GOOD NEWS PUBLISHERS

Just for Moms

Copyright © 1999 by Elizabeth M. Hoekstra
and M. Beth Cutaiar

Published by Crossway Books
      a division of Good News Publishers
      1300 Crescent Street
      Wheaton, Illinois 60187

Cover Photo: International Stock

Cover Design: Cindy Kiple

First printing 1999

Printed in the United States of America

Scripture taken from the *Holy Bible: New International Version*®.
Copyright © 1973, 1978, 1984 by International Bible Society.
Used by permission of Zondervan Publishing House. All rights
reserved.

The "NIV" and "New International Version" trademarks are
registered in the United States Patent and Trademark Office
by International Bible Society. Use of either trademark
requires the permission of International Bible Society.

Library of Congress Cataloging-in-Publication Data
Hoekstra, Elizabeth M., 1962-
   Just for moms : helping you and your daughter on her journey
to womanhood
      p.   cm.
   ISBN 1-58134-058-3 (tpb. : alk. paper)
   1. Parent and teenager. 2. Teenage girls. 3. Mothers and daughters.
4. Parenting--Religious aspects--Christianity.
I. Cutaiar, M. Beth, 1954- . II. Title.
HQ799.15.H64   1999
649'.133--dc21   98-45476
                                             CIP

12	11	10	09	08	07	06	05	04	03	02	01	00	99
15	14	13	12	11	10	9	8	7	6	5	4	3	2	1

CONTENTS

৯

Acknowledgments   7

Preface   9

1 What She Is Feeling   13

2 How to Talk with Her   25

3 Encourage Good Health Through Example   39

4 Talking About Her Body and Sexuality   53

5 Supporting Her during the 'Tween Years   75

Books You Might Enjoy   91

ACKNOWLEDGMENTS

Any book, but particularly books such as these that have been born of personal convictions, passions, and knowledge, are written as a result of numerous influences in the authors' lives. To name just a few: The greatest and humblest thanks goes to our Lord Jesus Christ. It was through God's grace and design for our respective lives that between the two of us, we have birthed six children. Carrying our children in utero and laboring to bring them into the world gave us each a pinnacle experience of femininity. Through our lives, the Lord prepared us in the many ways and gave us each the variety of experiences that in large and small ways contributed to *Just for Girls* and *Just for Moms.*

Our thanks also goes to our children. To Becky, Jennifer, Tom, Julie, Geneva, and Jordan—without each of you our lives would be incomplete. You have taught us much about ourselves in raising you. Thanks also to our husbands, Peter and Fred, for faithfully protecting and nurturing our femininity.

Our parents deserve all the credit for encouraging us in our personal beliefs and our interest in the medical field. I (Elizabeth) thank my parents, Tom and Cindy Marriner, for urging me and paying for me to earn my nursing degree. With that degree and knowledge grew a God-given passion for women's health. I (Beth) thank my parents, Karl and Merrily Wieland, for always encouraging me throughout life. And, Mom, thanks for your God-given zeal to insure that I was comfortable with my body as a young woman in puberty—not an easy task in the early 1960s!

With the invaluable help and guidance of our agent, Leslie Stobbe, we landed in the knowledgeable hands of Crossway Books. Thanks to each person at Crossway for the behind-the-scenes effort to bring these books to mothers and daughters. Thank you for believing in equipping young women to become adults who will have unwavering esteem for the persons God created them to be.

Our deepest thanks also goes to the young women and their moms who shared their histories and stories with us—particularly "Lori," "Sara," "Ellen," "Betsy," and their families. Thank you for your transparency.

Serving Him and for His glory,
Elizabeth M. Hoekstra and M. Beth Cutaiar

PREFACE

༄

Dear Moms:

As mothers of young women ourselves (Beth—a
mother to three women ages seventeen to twenty-
three, and Elizabeth—mother to a young woman
aged eleven), we looked for a book to meet our need
to equip our daughters for womanhood. Though
there are many wonderful books for teenage women
about sexual purity, the teen years are too late for
setting the stage for preadolescent women to
embrace their passage into womanhood. A preteen's
confidence is secured before her adolescent years by
equipping her with accurate, positive information
about the physical, emotional, and spiritual changes
she will be experiencing as she navigates puberty.

A preteen young woman needs Jesus and His
guiding hand as much now in her developing years
as later in her adult years. How she views herself
now in Christ will affect every other aspect of her
future. She must have a deep abiding faith in Jesus
Christ. She must have a full understanding and

respect for her body and how God designed it to function. She must have a high regard for her identity in the Lord. She must accept the truth that God made her a uniquely gifted woman to serve Him. These formative years in a young woman's passage to adulthood are so key to her long-term health that we couldn't put aside the idea that something *must* be written for them.

Compounding this conviction was our former extensive work for a pro-life Christian counseling center, where we counseled young women facing unexpected pregnancies. In our various tasks a deep compassion surfaced for young women who were ignorant of their bodies' workings and of God's plan for their lives. We felt deeply grieved. Already too many years had passed in these young women's lives. Patterns were set, mistakes had been made, self-concepts were tarnished. Our goal was always to introduce them to the saving grace of a personal relationship with Jesus Christ, and our deep desire was to reach them before the consequences of poor choices led them to knock on the counseling center's doors. We feel that the greatest gift we can give our own young women and your young woman is the threefold message of spiritual, emotional, and physical health. Womanly health is a lifelong, life-giving lifestyle. It is a pattern of behavior and thought processes that, with this book as a resource, you can teach your daughter.

Let us ask a question. How was womanly health information given to you? Did your mom have one talk with you? Did she give you a book to read? Did she let an older sister or cousin tell you "the facts of life?" Perhaps she was completely silent and let you figure the perplexing changes out on your own. Maybe your knowledge came in bits and pieces scattered over a number of years.

A good result of the sexual revolution in the 1970s was that we were given freedom to really begin to look at our bodies and how they work. With understanding came ownership; with ownership came self-acceptance; with self-acceptance came a desire to pass on good, accurate information to our daughters.

And that is where we are today.

Our guess is that you want to communicate better with your daughter about her womanhood than someone communicated with you. You know that your femininity and sexuality are privileges, and you want to pass this truth on to her. We've learned that silence is not the answer. Let's talk, and let's talk frankly with our daughters about who they are becoming as godly women!

We encourage you to read through *Just for Girls* before passing it on to your daughter. Then read it with your daughter, or assign a chapter at a time for her to read and then discuss it. Maybe you could buy her a special bookmark to keep track of her place while she's reading.

It will help your daughter adopt and embrace long-term womanly health if she takes ownership of her book. She needs to personalize the pages. We will encourage her to mark up the pages with her questions, thoughts, hearts, and stars. You, too, can help her make the book her own. Be sure she has the materials she needs to be able to do the various activities and follow the suggestions we offer her.

Keep her in prayer as she reads *Just for Girls*. Ask for God's direction and for open doors to discuss certain points with her. Pray for discernment to know when, how much, and what to discuss. Our prayer is that with *Just for Girls* and *Just for Moms* as resources, your relationship with your daughter will grow even stronger. Our hope is that she'll find you a reliable and trustworthy confidante during her trip into womanhood.

1

What She Is Feeling

Take heart, dear mother! Your daughter is growing into a young woman of God! Perhaps you've seen changes in her behavior that make you wonder where your charming little daughter has gone. Maybe she's pensive, moody, cranky, talkative, angry, bubbly, full of laughter, or silent—all in a matter of a few minutes. You may feel as though someone has kidnapped your child and replaced her with this impostor who is nearly unrecognizable—except, of course, she still has her father's eyes or her grandmother's legs or your laugh, etc. You know she belongs to you, but maybe you feel you are losing touch with who she is.

LORI'S MOM

꙳

Lori was moping around the house the other day. Every time I tried to talk to her, she either walked away or grumbled something I didn't hear clearly. I found myself gritting my teeth at her outright insolence and felt I couldn't take it another minute without yelling at her. I asked her to take the dog outside and told her when she came back inside, she had better have changed her attitude. I watched from the kitchen window as she half-heartedly threw a stick for the dog. The dog wanted to play harder, and when Lori didn't respond to his animated barks and running, he jumped up on her. She sprawled back onto her rear end. It was as if he had knocked the wind out of her because she just sat there. Then she curled her knees up to her chest and wrapped her arms around her legs. Thinking maybe the dog had hurt her, I trotted outside. As I approached, she began to rock back and forth, and I could see tears on her cheeks. The dog was thumping Lori's legs with his tail and trying to lick her tears. I bent down next to her and asked her if she was all right, but even before the words were all the way out of my mouth, she turned and wrapped her arms around my shoulders and buried her face in my neck. I felt stunned. Was this the same child that ten minutes ago couldn't stand to be in the same room with me?

I gently patted her back and asked again if she was okay, still thinking the dog had hurt her. She shook her head and said she wasn't hurt. Then she just blurted out that the reason she had been grumpy and mad at me was because the day before I had looked at her "funny" *when she had talked about a new pair of hiking boots she wanted to buy with her birthday money. I barely remembered the conversation, let alone my facial expression. But I took her at her word, apologized for my "funny look" that had obviously deeply hurt her feelings, and asked her to tell me again about the boots and why they would be special to her. We went and picked them out together the next day.*

ॐ

Has your daughter shown a similar extreme sensitivity over things you can't quite grasp? Young women entering puberty are exceptionally emotionally labile. You may feel as if you are always treading gently on her ego, trying not to bruise her spirit.

If you haven't already done so (and we do recommend that you read *Just for Girls*), read chapter 4, "It's a Whole New World." Look at each emotion we have listed. Do you recognize your daughter's emotions in any of these? Has she been able to verbalize any of these with you? You may want to go through the list with her and talk about each emotion and ask if she is feeling any of them. Maybe what she feels isn't listed, and she has written her own list. Encourage her to do that if she wants to. Remember there is no typical pattern for a preteen's development. Don't try to push her to conform nor compare her to her sisters or friends and their feelings or development.

It is helpful, however, for you to share with her your own memories of how you felt at the same age. Start with your spiritual life. Talk about how you came to know the Lord—even if it wasn't when you were a child. From there you can reflect back on how the Lord prepared you as a young teenager for the need of His presence in your life. If you truly can't remember your early teen years, employ the help of your parents or siblings. They may remember what you were like at that age (maybe too well!). Look through old photo albums, school yearbooks, letters, or journals—anything to help you remember.

We realize this activity could be extremely painful for anyone who may have been abused as a child. Sometimes watching your child reach the age at which you were abused causes your own pain to resurface. We recommend that you seek healing through a trained counselor, particularly if you have abuse issues that you've never talked about with anyone. If you do have a history of abuse, it is important to share this with your daughter in a general, nonfrightening way. You could explain to her that you want her growing-up years to be healthier than yours were.

A mother we know says she wanted to tell her daughter about being abused by an uncle when she was thirteen, the same age that her daughter was now. The woman was terrified that her family might find out. Yet she was even more fearful of her daughter being abused and wanted to warn her. She prayed for an appropriate time to share her story and pain with her daughter. When a divinely appointed opportunity arrived, she delicately informed her daughter about the abuse, and as they talked, her daughter began to cry. The girl confided that a boy in her eighth grade class had sexually assaulted her—a mom's worst nightmare! But in hindsight, after much prayer, forgiveness, and counseling, this mother says she is so thankful she initiated the conversation with her daughter. She's not sure her daughter would have ever told her about the assault otherwise.

Whether abuse is in your past or not, share positive and negative memories, explain how they made you feel, and how you resolved issues. Talk about mistakes you made and the consequences. The point of all this sharing is not to frighten your child, but to help her see you as a human being, someone who struggled like she does. This is your emotional connection. Because her feelings are new to her and she has become something of a foreigner to you, you need a new way to relate with her.

We are here to help you re-recognize your daughter. We want you to reestablish your connection with her now, *as the person she is becoming*, not as the child from a year or two ago. You are still very much needed as her parent and mother, but the key is to build on a solid, trusting relationship where communication is the binding cement.

Her physical, emotional, and spiritual needs have changed as her body is changing. You need to be able to talk with her about these changes. She needs your guidance and support more than ever, just in a more subtle way. Proverbs 22:6 says, "Train a child in the way he should go, and when he is old he will not turn from it." We trust you have done the best job you can "training" her so far, and she still needs more training, but you also need to trust her more to remember your training and ultimately the Lord's training. We know it's scary.

LIFE ON A KITE STRING

It's like flying a kite. Do you remember flying a kite as a child (or even as an adult)? You pieced together the fragile kite and gently wrapped the string on the spool. As you began to take a few steps into the wind, you let a little string out, and the kite played a few feet above your head. Then a moment of trepidation took over. You wanted to see the kite take flight, you wanted its bright colors to soar and cut through the breezes overhead, but you also wanted to keep it tethered close. What if it climbed on a gust and then lost its momentum and crashed to the ground? What if the string broke? What if the wind became so strong it pulled your kite right from your grasp and sent it soaring above your reach?

So it is with your prepubescent child. You know you need to give her more space, more room in which she can explore her limits. But you are frightened, and you know this is just the beginning of letting her grow into an adult and eventually releasing her altogether. Right now she needs your firm grasp on the strings of her life, but she also needs to find her own wind, to find her own lifting breeze where she can fly. At that safe spot she can dip and turn, exploring the air around her, remaining safely anchored to you.

A promise is offered in Psalm 91:11-12, and it seems particularly appropriate for parents fearful of their children's taking flight too soon. "For he will command his angels concerning you to guard you in all your ways; they will lift you up in their hands, so that you will not strike your foot against a stone." Indeed, the Lord will command His angels over your child, so she will not come crashing down or skittering across the hard ground. You cannot know His long-term plan for her, but you can know His plan is perfect and in her best interests. While she is fluttering about you, teasing on the kite string, be assured that He will remain as the sustaining wind under her.

During these times of her determined flight, you

will watch your daughter's inner tug of war between being a young girl and being a young woman. One minute she'll be giggling with happiness; the next she'll be crying over an infraction by her brother or sister. She's in the 'tween years, somewhere in the middle of being a little girl and a teenager. You'll see glimpses of your sweet, happy child, and you'll catch the wrath of a self-centered teenager. Her inconsistency will drive you crazy.

And that is your biggest clue to how to continue to relate to her. *You need to remain consistent.* You need to continue to protect her, to provide emotional support, to listen, even when she is yelling, crying, or laughing. Your stability and availability are essential to her growth. When your child was younger, there were generally rewards for all the giving you did—a knee hug, a sticky kiss, a crayoned picture, a "you're the best mom!" note. Now those may stop or lessen, but simultaneously you need to *increase* your giving attitude, without many rewards or recognition for your efforts. This is when parenting becomes deeply selfless.

You need to "be there" for her. Take her to the mall with her friends when she asks you to (not every day—agree on reasonable days and times). Go to her sporting events, help her stay involved in church youth programs, get involved in her school activities, volunteer in any clubs in which she is involved. Show a genuine interest in the things that interest her. Educate yourself about her hobbies. Better yet, do the hobby with her! A friend of ours goes outside and shoots basketball hoops with her fourteen-year-old daughter, despite the young woman being a full head taller than her mom. This mom has learned that dribbling the ball, shooting, and grabbing rebounds is a time of connection with her daughter. She has had some of the deepest, most rewarding conversations with her daughter under the basketball hoop. It doesn't matter that this mom misses more shots than she sinks. What matters is that she found a nonthreatening way to relate with her daughter.

You know why doing a sporting activity with your daughter isn't threatening to her? Because as you're active and talking together, you don't have to make eye contact. Yes, looking someone in the eyes when she's speaking shows her you are listening with interest, but eye contact with a young person who is struggling with her identity can make her feel overwhelmingly vulnerable. Doing a sport together diffuses intense conversations a bit, actually encouraging her to talk more freely.

Like our basketball-playing mom, when you take an interest in your daughter's life, when you reach beyond just parenting her and view her as a distinct person separate from you, it will draw her closer to you. Making an effort to enter her life will prove to her how much you care about her.

It's not easy, and there will be many days when you may think that you have failed her or yourself. There will be times of fear or terror when you release the string of her kite just a little, and she jerks against it for more freedom. There may be other times when she wants you to hold her tightly and not let her out of your grip. Listen to what she tells you, look for clues in how she is acting, learn to decipher her moods, be discerning and pray for wisdom in how to parent her, and build your relationship with her. She needs you as her biggest advocate in this, her journey into womanhood.

Action Points

☞ When your daughter is in a talkative mood, ask her what her "perfect day" would be like. How would she spend it? With whom? Her answers will tell you a lot about where her interests and priorities are right now.

☞ During another conversation ask her how she would like to spend a day with *you*. Shopping? Climbing a mountain? Reading on the beach? Set a date *right then* to do what she says. If her suggestion is out of the question, come to a compromise on which you both agree. Clear your schedule, and when the day comes, stick to your promise. Take pictures of whatever activity you are doing together, and when they are developed, give them to her in a little photo album. The pictures will remind her of your listening ears, your commitment to doing something with her, and your desire to remain a part of her life.

☞ Purchase a cloth-bound book of lined blank pages for her to use as a journal and a desk calendar for her to keep track of her periods.

2

How to Talk with Her

The fluctuating hormones surging through your daughter's body leave her perpetually premenstrual. She has little or no control over the normal rise and fall of these chemical messengers that act to balance her growth, development, and maturity of body organs. Even though she might not have started her periods yet, the hormones are in full swing.

She probably feels as if she is on a roller coaster. Yes, at the beginning she wanted to get in the coaster car. She wanted to go for the ride of her life, to feel the suspense of what's around the next corner, to find the end result of the mystery of womanhood. But as soon as the bar came down in front of her, locking her in place, she felt a little panicked. As the ride into adulthood jerked toward the top of the track, she felt moments of terror and yearned to go back. She looked behind her, jiggled the bar, even called back to you for help to get out, but she couldn't stop the coaster car. Now the car she is riding in is perched on the top rung, ready to fling her down steep slopes, around hair-raising curves, and even upside down. No wonder she is feeling a little out of control!

She may be out of control of the hormones raging inside her, but she is not out of control of how she reacts to them. It's easy to want to blame hormones for every foul mood, sarcastic attitude, and insolent remark. Be careful. Though hormones may well be the culprit of defiant behavior, to label her as "hormonal" almost gives her permission to keep behaving in an unacceptable manner. Yes, fluctuations will cause her to have very high highs and very low lows, but she still needs to be held accountable for her actions. She is growing older and more mature, and with that maturity comes responsibility.

She has school, friends, church, and family responsibilities that she must attend to in an acceptable fashion. Her family jobs may be just to keep her room clean, or maybe she helps with meal preparation and cleanup, or perhaps she is expected to care for her younger siblings. Regardless of what her family responsibilities are, you have somehow communicated your expectations to her. Whether these expectations have been spoken, written, or surmised, she knows what she is supposed to do.

NEW FORMS OF COMMUNICATION

Now as she begins her free fall into puberty, you may need to develop new ways of talking with her. Your once-verbal child may suddenly act as if she has lost her power of speech, and you need to locate and touch the nerve in her psyche that is still craving communication. Your goal is to develop a pattern of communication that involves her, that makes her feel as if she is getting more out of the conversation than you just talking *at* her. She wants to feel you are talking *with* her.

You've undoubtedly heard the adage that God gave us each one mouth and two ears so we could listen twice as much as we speak. It would've been even more obvious if He had given us three, four, or five ears—and still just one mouth! Think of how much better we might understand each other.

Despite having only two ears, listen, listen, and listen some more to your daughter. Allow her to voice whatever she wants, while you smile, nod, raise your eyebrows, mutter "uh-huh," and encourage her with your body language. But don't talk! Take notes if you feel you won't be able to keep your mouth shut. One inventive mom, who had a hard time not interrupting conversations with her daughter, found that setting the timer for five minutes gave her daughter time to talk. Mom listened to the ticking for five minutes, biting her tongue, but learned not to speak until the buzzer sounded. Then she would reset the timer for one minute, and allow herself one minute to ask questions or comment on what her daughter had said. It's a great ratio, five to one. Try it.

Encourage her to talk about whatever is on her mind, even if it seems trivial to you. If she wants to talk about it, obviously it is important to her. When she seems to have talked out her concern or what she is bubbling-over happy about, start asking good questions. What's a good question? One she can't answer with just a yes or no. Good, or open-ended, questions encourage her to keep talking, and the more she keeps talking, the more you will learn about her.

Proverbs 20:5 says, "The purposes of a man's heart are deep waters, but a man of understanding draws them out." Insert your respective names in the appropriate spots: "The purposes of my daughter's heart are deep waters, but I, as her mother, draw them out." Your daughter has very deep waters in her heart. She may even feel as if she is drowning in the confusing, dark depths. But you are uniquely qualified to be her life preserver. Your ears are the flotation device that will float her to the surface, keep her stable, and draw her to the safety of shore. All you have to do is *listen* for her cries and quiet whispers for help.

Sometimes these whispers are audible during teachable moments, those times when a question or issue comes up and opens the door to a thought-provoking conversation. Look and listen for hints that she might be open to a discussion. Read her body clues. Maybe she sighs every time she sees a billboard with a thin model sprawled across the frame. Perhaps she slouches in her chair every time a certain friend of her older brother is mentioned. Try to interpret her body language and then ask her open-ended questions.

You can initiate your own teachable moments with her too. Read one of her teen magazines and ask her what she thought about certain articles. Watch a movie or TV show with her that has some ethics that may be a little different from yours, and ask her how she would handle a similar situation. Read her history book and discuss with her how that portion of history is affecting her life right now. Pray for opportunities, times when the Lord puts you together in the right setting with some time on your hands to talk. Create moments when you have her undivided attention—riding in the car, waiting in line at the grocery store, walking the family dog— and talk with her.

GAINING TRUST

Through all this talking, you will be gaining her trust. She will come to see you as trustworthy. It's a different kind of trust than what she had when she was younger. When she was an infant, she cried, and you came. When she was a toddler, you fed her foods she wouldn't choke on. When she was in grade school, you bought her a bicycle helmet. She learned to trust that you would take care of her physical needs, that you would keep her safe. She learned she could count on you to protect her well-being. Now that she is a preteen or early teen, her trust in you begins to reach beyond meeting her physical needs. She needs to know she can trust her delicate emotions with you too and that what she says to you is kept private. You need to earn more of her trust by proving yourself trustworthy with her thoughts, ideas, and concerns. She needs to be assured that you will not share anything she has said to you with anyone else (unless you ask permission). You need to communicate to her that her ideas are valid, not silly or immature, and that they are of interest to you.

SARA'S MOM

With all the social activities Sara is involved in, she leads a very active life, yet there are times when I catch her looking wistful. Sometimes I'll see her hesitate in front of the living room window that looks out over the pond behind our house, and she'll just stare at it for a few minutes. She gets this blank look on her face, not smiling, not frowning, but a look of concentration, like she is trying to remember something. I want to know what she is thinking when she looks that way. Is she simply watching the wind play on the water? Does she want the peacefulness of the secluded pond? Is she remembering years past when we would toddle down there together and catch frogs? As a mother, am I reading too much into it?

The other day I was sorting through her clothes, weeding out the summer stuff to fit the winter sweaters in her dresser. I came across her journal—I know what it looks like because I gave it to her a couple of months ago. It's just a pink and purple cloth-bound book of empty pages, but it fanned out as I moved it, and I could see it was more than half full with her writing. I held it in my hands, rubbing the cloth. I turned it over and over. My fingers impatiently tapped on the binding. I wanted to read it; I wanted to see what she wrote; I wanted to know what was going on in my child's mind.

But I watched my hands snuggle the journal back between two T-shirts even as my mind said, "Wait." Then I turned and left her room. When she breezed into the house from school that afternoon, I told her I had started to clean out her drawers. A look of horror crossed her face as she realized I must have come across her journal. I just shook my head and smiled and told her I hadn't read it. She gave me a quick hug and dashed upstairs to her room.

I felt really proud of myself. I had been so tempted, but she would have known if I had read it. And I can only guess at the damage I would have done to our relationship. You know, two good things have come from this. One, I feel that she actually trusts me, respects me more, and, two, she cleaned out her dresser herself!

∾

Would you have been as trustworthy as Sara's mom? There may be times when you aren't even aware that you may be invading your child's privacy. In the past she wanted you to read everything she wrote, hang every picture she drew, listen to every conversation she had had with friends. Not so anymore. Even if she hasn't indicated that she wants more privacy, give it to her anyway. Don't read her journal or diary. Don't open her mail (even if you know it's a bill or something you will have to deal with). Don't eavesdrop on her telephone conversations, and don't snoop through her room. Offer her the same respect for her things and space that you have taught her to show for yours.

PRIVATE SPACE

Part of growing into a young woman of God is claiming her own space, marking her territory, proclaiming her independence. A twelve-year-old young woman we know told her mom she *couldn't stand* sharing a room any longer with her younger sister. Having limited space in the house, this mom wasn't sure quite how to fulfill her daughter's need for her own space and a little privacy. She came up with the idea of a "nest" and declared the space between her twelve-year-old's bedroom dresser and the wall as "off limits" to anyone but the twelve-year-old. She stuffed a bean bag chair into the corner and put a table lamp on the dresser. Now when her daughter is feeling that she needs a little privacy, she can be found snuggled in her nest, reading or drawing.

Tell your daughter you want to help her create a place of her own, sort of a refuge where she can feel safe. A place like this will give her feelings of security, comfort, and control. Her "nest" could be in her closet or a big, soft cushion on the floor in a secluded corner. While her body is changing, she needs the security of a familiar place where she can write, cry, read, or just daydream.

A secure spot designated as "private space" for your daughter will also give her a feeling of control.

So many other things in her life may seem out of control to her right now—particularly her body. There are times she may wish she could stop or at least delay her growth into a woman, but, of course, she can't. A private place to call her own gives her a sense of control of at least one thing in her life. It's like her own little kingdom where she can be governor.

WATCH YOUR TONGUE

During the metamorphosis of your daughter from a child to a young woman, remember to use positive language when you talk with her, especially about her body. Reread chapters 5 and 6 of *Just for Girls* to remind yourself of the concepts we tried to teach her about the changes in her life. Build up her confidence in herself and her changing body by using similar words and ideas.

James 3:9-10 says, "With the tongue we praise our Lord and Father, and with it we curse men, who have been made in God's likeness. Out of the same mouth come praise and cursing." Though this verse is generally interpreted as a reminder to use caution about what comes out of your mouth, we'd like to extend it to include how we talk about our own bodies. In chapter 5 of *Just for Girls* we talk to your daughter about being created in the likeness of God. Because God is the essence of beauty, your daughter can't help but be part of His beautiful creation too. Yet sometimes we "curse" His creation by using words and language that don't glorify Him or our human bodies.

How do you talk about your own and other people's bodies? Do you complain about how you look? Do you make comments about others who aren't attractive in your eyes? If you "curse" God's creation in this way, your daughter can't help but pick up on your attitudes. Try using only "praise" words to describe human bodies instead. Try words such as *attractive, lovely, gifted, exceptional, quality, modest, serene, radiant, glowing*—you get the idea.

So too with your daughter use only positive words when you talk about her changing body. Demeaning or sexist comments will only compromise her fledgling femininity. Her developing breasts are breasts, not boobs, or, pardon the expression, tits. Her prepubescent layer of fat deposits and muscle in her hips and buttocks are just that—temporary deposits, not "baby fat." Her growth of body hair doesn't make her a "monkey" but does prove the existence of puberty hormones. If you are uncomfortable saying "your period," use "your friend" or "monthly visitor," not "the curse," "on the rag," or "the monthly mess." Unfortunately, negative language will lead her to think of her femininity as dirty and undesirable, neither of which is even close to the truth!

Now, more than ever, she needs to hear how beautiful she is in your eyes, her father's eyes (more on her relationship with her dad in chapter 5), and God's eyes. Becoming a young woman is a radiant transformation, deserving of your encouraging remarks. Encourage her during *every* conversation you have with her. The adage goes "encourage ten times for every one time of constructive criticism." Build up her self-esteem by telling her what she is good at—even if you told her the same thing thirty times yesterday. Tell her you are confident of her ability to become a godly woman. Instill an attitude of reliance on her God-given gifts and skills. Talk about menstruation as an exciting turning point in her life and remind her that it is the whole physical foundation of womanhood.

You have a powerful resource to build up your daughter's confidence and esteem right at the tip of your tongue. Your encouraging spoken words combined with positive body language and attentive listening will help to keep the two-way line of communication wide open.

Action Points

☞ The spiritually wise book of Proverbs is packed with references to truthful speaking, the wayward tongue, damaging gossip, and careful listening. For the next month read one proverb a day. ("A proverb a day keeps the devil away".) Underline or highlight each passage applicable to bettering your communication with your daughter. Jot notes to yourself on how these verses could be applied to your everyday life. Memorize several verses that seem to address a specific area of communication in which you may have had a problem with your daughter. Pray for the Lord to give you opportunities to use what you have learned.

🕮 Take your daughter to a department store where she can pick out one or two oversized pillows and maybe a lap blanket to create her safe-spot nest. Allow her to decorate this small area as she pleases with posters, pictures, or photos. If space permits, give her a small lamp to use for reading and writing.

🕮 Purchase a devotional or spiritual meditation book for your daughter, one that appeals to her areas of interest.

3

Encourage Good Health
Through Example

Watching your daughter grow into a young woman is sometimes like watching a painfully slow rerun of your own life—because our children tend to copy us. They are like little camcorders from birth, so by the time they are young adults, they mimic and replay back to us many of our own thought processes, actions, mannerisms, and facial expressions.

You've seen the advertisements about the father holding a box of drugs, standing over his teenaged son saying, "Are these your drugs?" Then more angrily he demands, "Who taught you to use drugs?" And the son replies, "You! I learned it from watching you!" This is a powerful reminder to parents that what we do as adults, our children are likely to try or do. Smokers beget smokers; parents who don't wear helmets when riding bikes have children who won't or don't want to wear helmets when they ride bicycles.

As much as we may hate to admit it, our children are frequently our clones. And it's not fair for us to say or have the attitude: "Do as I say, not as I do." A mixed message hypocritically tells your child that you expect a higher standard of behavior from her than from yourself. Doesn't this leave a nearly imperceptible line between right and wrong?

Simply put, your actions not only speak louder than your words, but they scream for your child's attention. You are constantly under the watchful eyes of a very perceptive young lady. Ouch! Do you shudder at the thought of what she is "seeing" you do, or are you proud of the values and principles you are teaching without even opening your mouth? Francois de la Rochefoucauld said, "Nothing is so infectious as example." You have the opportunity to "infect" your daughter with your contagious example of how you care for yourself. Yes, a weighty responsibility, but also the privilege God has given you as her parent.

PATTERNS OF BEHAVIOR

Consider your unspoken thoughts about your own body. Does she see you grimace in front of the mirror or hear you complain about your body? Do your actions speak of an unhealthy attitude about food or eating? Do you tense at the mention of visiting a doctor, even for a "wellness checkup?" Do you abuse your body by not getting enough rest, by smoking, by poor eating habits, or by lack of exercise? Your attitudes about all these things tell your daughter you don't think your body is worth the effort of keeping it healthy. Forgive us if we speak intensely here, but isn't your daughter's long-term health (not to mention your own) worth a little effort? You have the ability to affect your daughter's health immensely. Is that something you want consciously to compromise?

Try to identify the areas in your life that could send a compromising message to your daughter about your womanly health or hers. Then take action to make changes.

Betsy's mom talks about her own struggles with her fear of doctors.

BETSY'S MOM

༈

I hate going to the doctor. I always have. When I'm sitting in the waiting room, I feel like I'm going to have a heart attack. My heart races, my mouth feels dry, my palms are sweaty. By the time I get into the office, my blood pressure is usually sky high.

The whole idea of someone examining me makes me feel so out of control. What if they find something wrong? What if I have to sneeze during my pap smear? What if I start to laugh from the cold stethoscope on my chest? It's all so embarrassing!

I feel like a child having such a strong dislike of the doctor, but that's exactly why I'm determined to get over this fear. I already see in Betsy the same panic every time she has to see the doctor. She is in excellent health because of all the sports she plays, but she has to have physicals fairly often to be on the teams. She chews on her nails in the waiting room and sits tensely on the edge of the chair. Have I done this to her? I don't want her growing up to be terrified of doctors. I want her to know that the doctor is her advocate for good health.

I want to be able to apply that to my own life!

✧

Betsy's mom is keenly aware that her reaction to visiting a doctor has been "inherited" by Betsy. Betsy hasn't inherited a dislike of doctors genetically, but has picked up on her mother's discomfort simply by her mom's actions and attitudes.

How can Betsy's mom change her own attitudes and help Betsy start to view visits to the doctor more positively? They can both start by talking about why they even go and see the doctor. Visits for annual physicals are for prevention, a screening process to catch an illness or disease before it happens. It's too late to close the barn door after the horse has run off. The time to prevent the horse from exploring on his own is while he is in the barn. Close the door. So it is with doctors. The way to prevent an illness is by seeing the doctor—before an illness even crops up. Indeed, an ounce of prevention is worth a pound of cure.

Talk with your daughter about why she needs to see the doctor regularly. Also talk with her about your own feelings—even if you are somewhat fearful of going to the doctor. But then explain to her that you want her to develop good life-long habits, and you are trying to change your fears about seeing a doctor.

God has entrusted you and your daughter with your earthly bodies. With His trust He asks you each to care for your body in a way that is honoring to Him. First Corinthians 6:19-20 says, in part, "Do you not know that your body is a temple of the Holy Spirit, who is in you, whom you have received from God? . . . Therefore honor God with your body." In short, your body is one of the most precious possessions God has given to you as a woman! You need to take precautionary measures now, regardless of your age, past patterns, or mistakes, for your extended good health.

Education and knowledge are the keys to helping you and your daughter feel comfortable with your bodies, giving you both the desire and ability to embrace long-term emotional, spiritual, and physical health.

In chapters 7 and 9 in *Just for Girls* we covered all the basics about a young woman's maturing body. Your body as an adult isn't too much different. If the way your body is designed and functions is a bit hazy to you, go back over these two chapters. Once you have a clear understanding and are armed with accurate information about your own body, you'll feel more comfortable talking to your daughter about hers.

Be sure when you are talking with your daughter to use correct terminology for her body parts. Slang words are at best confusing and are generally degrading. If you consistently speak the same language about your daughter's body, she will become comfortable with the terms too—a win-win situation for both of you. Use the terminology from her book or borrow a medical dictionary from the library to be certain of accuracy.

PROTECTING HER MODESTY

Your daughter may already feel quite modest and shy about her body—the evidence being baggy sweatshirts, sweaters, and pants. Another young woman may be very aware of her shapely figure and want to show it off a little. Either way her modesty needs to be protected.

Some girls develop modesty naturally at a fairly young age—seven or eight. Others need to be taught about modesty. Modesty is different from shame. A young woman may be embarrassed and wish to hide her body because she is ashamed of it. We've spent a lot of time trying to help your daughter not be ashamed of her body, but rather respect it! Modesty is a desire to protect the body from public view. You encourage modesty when you teach your daughter to sit with her legs crossed if she is wearing a dress rather than sitting spread eagle. Modesty is wearing a swimsuit that covers most of her breasts. It is not wearing such short shorts that her buttocks are hanging out. It is respecting her body enough to keep it covered in public. Modesty also means wearing a girl's T-shirt as her breasts are starting to develop and a bra as she grows larger breasts. Especially if she is involved in sports, a bra will not only provide modesty but will offer some support and protection.

Do you know why God made men and women with pubic hair? Partly for protection but also as a covering for modesty. A woman's pubic area and breasts are areas of great vulnerability—to germs and trauma, yet these are the avenue to the greatest intimacy a man and woman can share. He made certain parts of your daughter's body to be kept private until she is married. You can teach her modesty by instructing her about appropriate clothes and how to sit, stand, and walk in public.

Your daughter may not have expressed a need for modesty yet, but take the initiative and look for ways you can teach her and help her to protect her modesty and privacy.

Ellen's mom tells of her experience, discovering too late Ellen's need for privacy.

ELLEN'S MOM

⌁

We've always been very open in our house. When Ellen and her brother were little, we weren't shy about seeing one another naked. Ellen's reaching puberty changed all that! Her father and I didn't catch on quickly enough though. I'm afraid Ellen felt humiliated by something that happened a couple of months ago. It showed us how much privacy she needs.

I had been after Ellen's dad to put a lock on the bathroom door—the only bathroom in the house. He hadn't seen a need for it, especially since in the morning when we all are rushing to get ready at the same time, very often one of us would be using the shower while another would be using the sink. But Ellen had asked even me to stop using the bathroom when she was in there. I guess I didn't recognize the seriousness of her request. One day her dad walked into the bathroom just as she was stepping out of the shower. He hadn't meant to barge in on her. He didn't think much of it until she became nearly hysterical. She knows that I know she is sensitive about her body, so she blamed me for not making sure her dad put a lock on the door. She felt completely humiliated. She cried about her lack of privacy and begged me to promise it wouldn't happen again.

You can be sure I went and bought a lock and had it installed right away. I've apologized to her for not seeing her need for privacy sooner, but I know she still feels embarrassed about what happened.

෴

In your own family, don't wait until something happens that embarrasses your daughter. Start ensuring her privacy now. Install locks on bathroom doors; allow her a lock on her bedroom door; make it a house rule always to knock on any closed door before entering. Talk about ways you can protect every family member's privacy.

MODELING CHRIST

Naturally an integral part of your overall health is your walk with the Lord—or maybe we should say your *marathon* when you're raising children! Each mom reading this can undoubtedly testify that a relationship with Jesus Christ is the glue that holds together every other aspect of her health. When a woman suffers emotional pain, she cries out to the

Lord for understanding; when she has physical discomfort, she seeks healing from God; when she has questions about how to mother her children, she asks for wisdom. He is the one who hears all her requests and meets all her needs.

The question is, does your daughter see you asking the Lord for guidance? Does she hear, see, and feel your personal relationship with Jesus Christ? A woman's faith is very private and intimate, yet a mother needs to communicate it to her daughter. You need to model the truth that a personal relationship with Christ is *the only answer* to life's challenges. Also recognize that during these years, some young teens may start to question your beliefs and their own beliefs. Your modeling may have to be subtle. How? Let her see you read the Bible every day, pray out loud for her even if she'll only allow it at the supper table, tell her of how the Lord has answered your prayers, exude Christ's love, patience, and compassion.

A young mom we know, Erin, tells of how, when she was a young teenager, her mother's unusual expression of faith had an impact on her life. At thirteen Erin had been sent to a private boarding school and hated every minute of the confining atmosphere. She wrote home weekly begging her parents to let her come home. She says that initially her mom responded with long letters about God's will and His wisdom. Erin hated and resented the letters; the written words meant nothing to her. Her mom's epistles, as she liked to call them, made her feel that not only were her parents not listening to her, but God was ignoring her too. Then her mom wisely stopped writing letters. Instead she started sending her daughter simple line drawings of sheep, a shepherd, rainbows, the cross on a hill, Noah's ark, trees and sky. This young mom now says those pictures meant more to her during the lonely times away at school than any words her mom could have written. The simplicity of God's faithfulness in the drawings spoke volumes to the isolated young woman searching for any evidence of God in her life.

As this wise mother did many years ago, you too can look for ways that will minister to and speak to your child. If she's artistic, tell her of God through pictures, drawings, or photos. If she loves nature, collect items from a park or the woods that remind you of God and share them with her. If she is musical, buy her Christian tapes (by musicians she likes). If she likes to read, buy her spiritual meditation books or Christian poetry geared for young people. Once again, you are meeting her where she is on *her* journey with the Lord, with instruments that will guide and direct her as an individual. Through this you are showing her that her Christian walk is important to you, and yet you respect the speed and the route on which she is traveling.

Your own examples of a personal relationship with Jesus Christ, using accurate language, conscientious body care, good eating habits, daily exercise, and a positive self-image will teach your daughter the same healthy attitudes, without your nagging or even saying a word! She'll be able to see the effects of these healthy habits in how you look, feel, relate to others, and feel about yourself. When these are instilled at a young enough age, they will become a permanent part of her life. She'll seek time with the Lord. She'll have a healthy diet without even thinking about it. She'll get daily exercise. She'll have a clear understanding of her body's workings. *She'll feel good about herself.*

And that is the whole purpose of these books! If we could grant one ideal to your daughter, it would be a good self-image and sense of her worth as a child of God. With a positive, God-centered self-image, she will be able to stand tall (figuratively and literally) in her personal faith and in the knowledge of what she is becoming.

Action Points

⌦ Educate yourself and keep up with medical news by subscribing to a women's health periodical. Leave issues lying around the house—on the coffee table, in the bathroom, next to the computer. Your daughter may pick them up to read when you aren't looking!

☞ Purchase T-shirts for your daughter, even if she doesn't have evidence of breasts yet. If she does have small breasts, use a tape measure to help her determine what size bras to buy.

☞ If you haven't already, consider switching your daughter to a female doctor or nurse practitioner. When setting up appointments for your daughter to visit the doctor, make them during her "best" time of day (i.e., if she is a morning person, pull her from school for a morning visit). Make the visit a rewarding experience—promise a bagel and tea at the local coffee shop after the visit or take her to her favorite clothing store.

☞ Keep a prayer journal together. List her prayer requests (*anything* she wants to pray for) and your own pertaining to her. Pray at least weekly together for items on the list and record how and when God answers the prayers.

☞ If you struggle with a low self-image, try to boost your confidence by reading books about who you are in God and about fulfilling your godly position as a woman. (See the "Books You Might Enjoy" list at the back of this book.)

4

Talking About Her Body and Sexuality

Your daughter is a sexual being. This can be one of the hardest things for parents of a young woman to realize and accept. Perhaps it's hard for you to think of her "that way." But from our births God created us to be sexual beings. His first directive to Adam and Eve was to have intercourse so they would reproduce: "God blessed them and said to them, 'Be fruitful and increase in number; fill the earth and subdue it'" (Genesis 1:28).

God's design is also for young men and women to *grow into* their sexuality. They are sexual beings from the start, but they don't necessarily have sexual feelings from the start. The sexual feelings, or the acute awareness of the opposite sex, may start as early as nine or ten or may not be noticeable until young people are around fourteen. The influences that will determine when your daughter starts to have sexual feelings is part nature and part nurture.

NATURE VERSUS NURTURE

Hormones, the chemical mail messengers we talked about in chapter 2 of this book and in chapter 8 of *Just for Girls,* have probably only about a 50 percent influence on your daughter's developing sexuality. The hormones do dictate when certain events will happen in her body—all of which will take several years to complete. As we all know, and what needs to be reiterated to your daughter, is that we cannot rush nature nor can we slow it down. How she is developing and the rate at which she is developing was predetermined by God Himself.

Also, young women in this country are maturing faster now than ever before in history. Several theories explain this. One is that over the last several decades, nutrition has improved so dramatically that young women's bodies are healthier as they enter their early teens. The improved overall health has encouraged their bodies to mature more quickly. Another theory looks at the increase in hormones in the meat we consume. The growth hormones fed to cattle is stored in their muscles, and small amounts are still in the meat when we cook it. Some researchers say the ingestion of secondhand hormones in this way has caused puberty to occur earlier.

Despite the earlier onset of puberty, almost all young women will feel that their bodies are developing at the *wrong* rate. Of course, there really is no *right* rate, but your daughter may remain unconvinced. She may feel as though her body is doing things backwards, too slowly, too fast, out-of-order, or completely insufficiently. She may compare herself to friends and feel she is lacking or too advanced in some areas—whether it is breast development, the start of her periods, growth of pubic hair, or being shorter or taller than other young women.

After reading *Just for Girls*, she'll have a clearer picture of God's perfect timing for her. She'll have confidence in her developing womanly health. It will also help to remind your daughter that every hair on her head (and every other part of her body) is numbered by the Lord. "And even the very hairs of your head are all numbered" (Matthew 10:30). He knows your daughter that intimately. And because of this intimate knowledge, He knows exactly what the best timing is for her body to develop.

The other influence in your daughter's growing sexuality is nurture, i.e., the influences in her environment. Let's face it—as parents attempting to keep our children pure, we are pitted against a sexually saturated culture. Everywhere our children go, they are bombarded with sex. Even prime-time "family" television shows are loaded with sexual innuendos. In school your daughter may be surrounded by peers who have had little moral training. Even Christian-schooled children and home-educated children cannot be completely sheltered from lower standards of behavior. They are simply everywhere!

Many young women seem to display sexual precociousness, or an understanding beyond their physical years due to exposure to the media and peers. If you notice your daughter using words and phrases that seem inappropriate for her age, these may just be terms she has heard others use and is trying them out for herself. She may want to see what kind of reaction she'll get from you. Using sexual phrases doesn't necessarily mean she knows what they mean or that she has experienced sexual situations. At nine, ten, or eleven years old, she probably doesn't even have sexual feelings yet. To her these are just terms or words. However, if you have cause for concern that she has been in a sexual situation (i.e., sudden depression, stained underwear, more than normal regressive behavior, inappropriate sexual behavior or knowledge, calling herself "dirty," exhibiting eating disorders, or bladder infections), she needs to be evaluated by a professional for sexual abuse. Any of these signs could be attributed to a number of other things or to nothing at all. Don't panic. Talk with her and get help if you need to.

THE "BIG TALK" VERSUS TEACHABLE MOMENTS

Even if up to this point you've avoided talking with your daughter about intimate relationships between men and women, you can still start now. Though it's optimal if you've set the stage in the past by talking openly about your femininity and sexuality, it's not too late to start bringing up the subject with frequency from now on.

The important thing is to find out what your daughter already knows about sexual relationships. Ask her if she understands the meaning of the words and phrases she hears or knows. She might not have a clue—she just knows that whenever she says certain words, she gets a reaction from people! Other young women might be so naive they still think storks bring babies. But it's essential to know what she knows. As the saying goes, there are two types of information your daughter will get about sex—correct information and incorrect information. Therefore, your job is twofold: Be sure she has accurate information and amend any misinformation she has been given.

Don't wait for her to come to you with questions. Some young women may have many unclear thoughts and aren't able to form them into a ques-

tion. Their questions are more like fleeting ideas.
Take the initiative. Just going through *Just for Girls*
together is a great basis for conversation starters.

She needs to know you are available to her for
any question she may have. She may ask you the
same question five different ways—directly and
indirectly. Your consistency in teaching her the right
answer not only reaffirms the truth but confirms you
are always available for questions and answers.
What if she asks you a question you don't know the
answer to? Don't worry—it's better to be truthful
and agree to look it up for her than to make up an
answer or let the question go unanswered. You
never know what you'll learn from her questions. If
she is your first or only daughter, of course there will
be times that you may be stumped, but find out the
answer and get back to her as quickly as possible.
From this she is not only gaining valuable information that she needs, but she is learning that she is
important to you and that you are a reliable resource
for answers.

When you do respond to her questions and
you're not sure how much information to give her,
start with the simplest, most basic answer. Betsy's
mom tells of a time when she answered a question
eleven-year-old Betsy asked about sex.

BETSY'S MOM

❧

Betsy came to me after school one day and asked me what "screwing" meant. I answered that it meant using a screwdriver to twist a screw into a piece of wood to hold two pieces of wood together. She sighed and said, "I know that, Mom. I meant, you know, screwing."

I admit I was shocked. My first impulse was to tell her never to use that term again and ask where she heard it in the first place. But then I realized that if I overreacted, she wouldn't feel safe to come to me again with questions. Besides, I wanted to know what she thought it meant. She said she thought it meant something about sex. I told her that, yes, it did, but that that term was an impolite word to use for something that God created for a husband and wife to enjoy together.

Then I asked her if she understood what sexual intercourse meant between two people. She nodded shyly. But she didn't turn away, so I figured I had a great opportunity to do a little teaching. I told her just the basics—that when husband and wife want to show each other how much they love each other, the husband inserts his erect penis into her vagina, and they move around together until they both feel an intense physical pleasure.

Then I asked her if I had answered her question. She mumbled, "Yes," and started to turn away. But then she turned back and said, "But why do they call it screwing?" I just wanted to remove that word from her vocabulary! But I again bit my tongue and said that it's because when the husband and wife are together, the husband does move his penis in and out of his wife's vagina and, yes, it does have similarities to the carpenter's term. But then I strongly reiterated that it was not an appropriate term for a married couple because sexual intercourse is done out of love and a desire to please one another, not a term or act used by builders. I asked again if I had answered her question, and this time she nodded confidently and trotted upstairs.

ﾌ

What a great response to Betsy's question! Her mom chose the most basic answer first. When that wasn't enough, she added more. When that wasn't enough, she continued until Betsy was satisfied with the answer.

All information you give your daughter about sexual intimacy should be followed by two questions of your own. First, "Did I answer the question you were asking me?" If she says no, give the same explanation with a few more details and repeat the first question. Keep giving her information in small doses until she says that you have answered her original question. You know best how much information your child can handle. There are some twelve-year-olds who do not want to know all the details, but there may be some nine-year-olds who have to know everything. Go with your instincts and pay attention to your daughter's body language. She'll start to shut you out physically if you're giving her too much information. If she's on overload, she'll turn away, cross her arms, withdraw, avoid eye contact, cry, etc. Let her tell you how much she wants to know.

Following every conversation the second question to ask your daughter is: "Do you have any other questions?" She may not have any more right away, but assure her that she can ask you anything anytime. In a few days, ask her if she's had any more thoughts or questions about what you discussed earlier.

Talking to your daughter about sex is not something you do just once or twice. It's an ongoing conversation. The how, when, where, and what you say will be affected by your own comfort level. We realize some moms of the nineties were raised in the fifties—right before the sexual revolution. Though those homes were filled with love and security, they were also homes where you just didn't talk about these personal things.

But you know what is so exciting? With you and your daughter's generation that silence can be broken! Your honesty and up-front attitude about sexuality and body image can set a new standard for openness and honesty. Right now you are equipping your daughter to be a mother to her own daughter someday. What a wonderful privilege! You can positively influence your future granddaughter right now by helping your daughter to have healthy, accurate information about her body and sexuality!

Research has shown that one of the most consistent factors pushing a young woman toward having sexual relationships and becoming pregnant outside of marriage is lack of education. This doesn't mean we should subscribe to the "safe-sex" campaign, but it does mean that we have a responsibility to teach our daughters why and how not to have premarital sex. It starts with her having such a high esteem of her body and sexuality that she wouldn't even consider defiling it before she is married. Your day-to-day interaction with your daughter will model positive lifestyle choices for her. How you present your own values, sexuality, and body image will subliminally seep into her subconscious.

YOUR OWN FEMININITY AND SEXUALITY

One of the first questions you need to answer is, are you comfortable with your own sexuality? If you aren't, it's okay! It doesn't mean you'll fail at instructing your daughter. By simply reading this book, you've made a giant step in becoming more comfortable with your own sexual identity and your daughter's. (See the book list at the back of the book for helpful resources in gaining understanding about female sexuality.)

A good place to start introducing femininity is by making your own femininity obvious. Talk openly about your period or feeling premenstrual. Menstruation is not a secret. She's probably already figured out when you're crabby that you're about to menstruate. Mark your periods on the family calendar (this is great for your sons too—it teaches them something they'll need to know about their future wives). Take your daughter shopping with you and have her find your chosen form of feminine protection on the shelf. Let her see the different types of boxes and choices. Right there in the grocery store have her handle the different boxes. In a sense you are ending the mystery about these items. She needs to be able to make these simple choices for herself someday. Watching you and discussing the purchase openly with you will help her.

Talk with your daughter about your own periods and feminine health too—how they have changed over the years, what they were like when you were her age, what your first one was like, any times you got caught off guard. Talk to her about when you became pregnant with her, when you knew, how you found out, how it made you feel, how you told her father. Tell her about when she was born, what day of the week it was, what you were doing when you went into labor, what you felt the minute she was born, what she looked like when she was born.

Also let her handle your bras—simply by asking her to wash them for you or fold them. Show her how to clasp and unclasp them. Teach her how the shoulder straps adjust. Measure yourself for a bra while she watches. Then measure her. Bring her to the lingerie department of a store and let her see and touch the different choices, materials, and styles. Ask her which ones she likes the best and why.

Do you know what you're doing through all of this? You're presenting yourself as a sexual, feminine *woman*. You're not just "Mom" anymore. You're a co-participant in womanhood!

HER FEMININITY

Traditionally a girl's first period earmarks her passage into womanhood. But in reality her passage started years earlier when she started getting a body odor and her feet grew at a tremendous rate.

If you suspect that your daughter may be shy about telling you when her period starts, look for clues—pink-stained underwear or her sudden desire to wash her underwear herself. Check the box of tampons or pads that you've bought her; watch for rolled up pads in the trash. If you find evidence, casually ask her if she's started. If she's shy, let her be shy about it. Don't call all your friends and report the news. On the other hand, some young women will have been waiting so anxiously for the day of their first periods that they'll be on the phone reporting it to everyone themselves. The point is to allow your daughter to stay true to her God-given personality as she deals with her first few periods. You've lived with her for about twelve years. You know best how to encourage her and support her. She may not want her dad or brothers to know. Respect her wishes.

The physical changes your daughter is experiencing may catch her off guard and scare her. Lori's mom tells of a time recently when Lori came to her in tears because she had a "lump" on her chest.

LORI'S MOM

✂

Lori had been outside playing and came into the kitchen in tears. I figured she had bumped herself, knowing how sensitive to pain she is. She cries very easily. When I asked her what had happened, she wailed, "I have a lump, and it hurts!" When I asked her where, she placed her hand over the left side of her chest. I asked if I could look, and she nodded. She wiped her eyes and pulled up her shirt. I didn't see anything, so I asked her to touch where it hurts. She gingerly touched her nipple. I asked if I could touch the spot too. Lower lip pouting, she nodded again. I gently touched her left nipple, and sure enough there was a little lump about the size of a grape. She winced. I pulled her shirt back down and smiled. "It's your breast bud, honey," I assured her. "It just means you're becoming a woman."

"But I don't want to!" she wailed again.

I gathered her into my lap and rocked her for a minute. "Why not?" I asked. She shrugged. "Do you want to stay a little girl a little longer?" I asked. She sniffled and nodded again. "Well, I think you've got some more time to be a little girl. This doesn't mean you're going to turn into a woman tomorrow. Okay?"

She smiled and pushed away from me. "I'm going to go back outside now."

I nodded and watched her trot out the door, ponytail bobbing on her back.

Developing breasts is a very big deal to young women! You may not remember the agony and despair you likely experienced as a young woman about your growing breasts. But you'll just as likely relive it with your daughter.

Young women's breasts do at first appear as little "breast buds." As Lori found out, they can be very tender to the touch. It's not at all unusual for one breast bud to appear weeks before the other. Frequently the young woman's dominant side (right-hand or left-hand) will show breast development first, and that breast may remain slightly larger throughout her adult life. To a young woman though, this can be a point of extreme embarrassment. To her, it seems that one breast is of a *hugely* different size and proportion than the other. In reality, it's most noticeable from her vantage point of looking down than from someone else's. Encourage her to stand in front of a mirror and see the difference. Also, if she wears loose-fitting clothing, it will be even less noticeable. Assure her that the breasts will become more even as time goes on. In the meantime though, be very sensitive to her worry about "abnormal" breast growth. It may be the focal point of her thoughts for a time.

HER SEXUALITY

During these early changes, at nine, ten, or eleven years old, a girl likely doesn't have sexual feelings yet, other than possibly noticing that when she bathes, a certain spot on her vulva feels good when she touches it. But this is not associated with sex or with thoughts of the opposite sex.

The challenge of presenting the act of sexual intercourse to your daughter can be intimidating. Reread how we explain it to her in chapter 12 of *Just for Girls.* You can paraphrase how we wrote it or add little bits and pieces to what we wrote. Maybe read it out loud with her, or ask her to read it silently. Then discuss it.

What and how much you tell your daughter will depend on her *emotional* age. And only you can be the judge of that. As we've said before, some nine-year-olds are ready and need to hear all the details, and there may be some thirteen-year-olds who aren't ready. Watch her body language to see if she's able to hear more or if she's on overload and tuning you out.

When you decide to approach her, be sure it is on "her turf," someplace where she feels comfortable—perhaps her bedroom, your bedroom, while driving in the car, or while out for a walk. Pick a place where you know you won't be interrupted and where you can keep your body language open and receptive to her. If you appear tense and nervous, her radar will pick up on it, and she'll be tense and nervous. On the other hand, if you are nervous, it's okay to say so. Just explain that the subject of a husband and wife's intimate relationship is a very private thing, and you don't talk about it very often. Follow that with a big *BUT*, saying that because you value her so much and want to be sure she has good and accurate information, you're willing to put your shyness aside to teach her about a married couple's intimate relationship.

Remember to include her in the conversation. Ask her if she understands what the terms you use mean. Have a dictionary handy or a women's health book in case you need to look things up together. Let her interrupt you with questions, and ask her if she has any questions. Remind her that you'll be discussing this again. She doesn't have to grasp it all right now.

She may wonder how she fits into all of this. After all, she may want to just go outside to play and ride her bike. Boys? Yuck! To her sex may seem very foreign and very far off. In a way it is, and consider yourself blessed if she remains impervious to boy/girl tensions for a while. But in another way it's not very far off at all. Before either of you realize it, she will begin to have primary sexual feelings that she may not even recognize as such. Maybe she'll feel giggly or shy around boys. Maybe she'll blush when she sees a man and woman kiss on TV.

Again it may be hard to recognize your daughter as a sexual being, but, face it, she is. It's essential that you do acknowledge this. You can't downplay her sexual feelings once she starts to have them. She may not have sexual feelings for a number of years, but she must know what to do with those feelings once they start. She may feel frightened of her feelings of attraction toward young men, or she may be delighted. Both, and anything in between, are nor-

mal responses to awakening sexuality. The differences in various young women's reactions aren't
anything you can predict, but you can plan for them.

Try reading Proverbs 5:15-23 together. Ask her if
she understands the analogy presented here.
"Running water," "springs," "streams of water,"
"fountain"—all pertain to the life-giving fluids from
a man's and a woman's bodies. The admonishment
to keep them to yourself and your spouse is for protection from sin and the consequences of sin. Song of
Solomon also offers a reverberating seductive poem
of this same sentiment: Adore your marriage part-
ner and stay pure with him alone.

In chapter 13 of *Just for Girls* we discussed with
your daughter ways to stay safe, and we talked
about not sharing items with people. It's the same
strategy here—no sharing of your sexuality with
anyone but your husband.

Your daughter's reaction to all of this information will tell you when to stop this conversation and
when to pick it up again. She may laugh through
your whole talk; she may sit silently and just nod.
She might cry, or she might interrupt so often with
questions that you're barely finishing sentences. All
reactions are fine. What's important to remember is
that there is no "guaranteed formula" you can use
that will always work. You need to be flexible and
sensitive to your daughter. Even if she completely

blocks you out during your first attempt, try again soon. Keep bringing up the topic every several weeks or so until you are satisfied that she knows what she needs to know for this time in her life.

MAKING ALLIES AT HER SCHOOL

Sex education is being introduced earlier and earlier in school systems. As early as third and fourth grade your daughter is introduced to anatomy, making good choices, saying no, etc. Some schools are pushing the "safe-sex" agenda, theorizing if we educate about birth control and condoms, we'll eliminate pregnancy and venereal diseases. Others are sticking with abstinence-based programs, recognizing that saying no is the only true protection from the consequences of sex outside of marriage. Either way you cannot depend on the school as the only and complete source of sexual education for your daughter.

Think of the school more as an adjunct to your primary teaching—not the other way around. Your daughter's initial introduction to sex education must begin at home. It is not only your role to talk with your daughter about these things, but it's your privilege too. Influencing her at home with your morals, standards, and values will help her to take school information and assimilate it according to what you have already taught her.

At the same time, however, the school is not your enemy nor necessarily even a threat to what you are teaching your daughter. Think of your relationship with her school as co-laboring to equip your daughter with accurate information. Yes, you may need to put the teaching she receives into a Christian context, but the information they have is medically accurate.

This co-laborer approach capitalizes on the saying, "You can love your child's teachers to you, or you can drive them away." The idea is to develop a healthy working relationship *with* your daughter's teachers and principal. How? Become their ally—build a relationship with them. Show that you care about the school, be active in school events and activities. Show your face and use your talents in the school system. Volunteer as a room mother or assist the school secretary with clerical work for a couple of hours each week. Join the PTA, chaperone field trips, or cook for holiday parties.

Remember to be genuine in this. You're not there as a spy; you're there to improve the quality of your child's and other children's education. A servant's heart will earn the respect of the staff. You aren't there to make them change; you're there to help them do their jobs. See the difference? Your goal isn't to manipulate them but to assist them. As your credibility increases with teachers and principals, your voice can be heard. You may be able to influence them to look at other curriculums to add to what they have, or you might be able to suggest another approach. This is shaky ground though. You can't be subversive—they'll see through it in a heartbeat! Be honest with them always. If they say no to your suggestions, be thankful that at least they listened to your concerns. They may not alter anything, but you have their respect. Keep praying for them and about your concerns. And above all, keep working willingly with them. They will begin to see you as a valuable resource—as opposed to a watchdog.

When you've developed a positive relationship with the school, and you then ask to see the curriculum for their sex education classes, they aren't going to feel threatened. They'll know it's because you care. With an advance understanding of the curriculum your daughter will be taught, you now are armed to teach her at home first. Dilute information you think unnecessary for her to learn. Talk about what the school will be teaching and redirect it with your Christian values. After the class ask her if she has any questions. Ask her how her Christian beliefs tie into what she learned. In this way show her that you are working with the school to teach her.

Your daughter may feel that with this constant looking at femininity and sexuality, all she wants to do is stay a child. It all may sound very complicated to her. Remember that the key to teaching your daughter about her body and sexuality is to *listen to her*. Pace imparting of information to her needs and individuality. She doesn't need to know everything now. Just as her body is taking years to mature, complete information will take years for her to absorb.

Action Points

☞ Plot out your periods for several months on the family calendar. Show your daughter your menstrual pattern, and encourage her to use her calendar the way we taught her in chapter 10 of *Just for Girls*. An interesting scientific note: When women live together, their bodies very often take on the same biorhythms, meaning they will frequently have the same menstrual pattern. See if this happens with your daughter.

☞ Memorize Psalm 139:13-16 together. These are powerful verses—particularly when read or recited aloud by children. Practice saying the verses with each other. Perhaps recite them together at a women's retreat, on Pro-life Sunday at your church, or during other church events.

5

Supporting Her During the 'Tween Years

The Lord has a special place in His heart for moms and dads struggling to raise godly children. He knows you value the privilege of raising the children He has given you. He can right the errors parents unwittingly make in parenting; He can restore relationships with your children if there has already been damage; He forgives your human failings in dealing with your children. He wants you to do the best job you can, seeking His guidance daily.

Isaiah 40:11 is a "mothering verse": "He tends his flock like a shepherd: He gathers the lambs in his arms and carries them close to his heart; he gently leads those that have young." Once again Christian parents are the sheep, quietly coaxed along by Him, The Great Shepherd. "He gently leads those that have young." The word *gently* is so reassuring. God understands a mom's confusion and feelings of inadequacy in raising her children so well that He tenderly and lovingly leads her along.

PARENTING WISDOM

The Lord supports moms and dads in their parenting roles. He is the ultimate parent to parents—full of wisdom, patience, grace, mercy, loving discipline, and forgiveness. We can *ask* for the same wisdom that He uses to deal with us. The wisdom we need as parents, a reflection of His own wisdom, is described in James 3:17: "But the wisdom that comes from heaven is first of all pure; then peace-loving, considerate, submissive, full of mercy and good fruit, impartial and sincere." That's a lot to live up to as a parent! Let's look at it more closely in the context of relating to your child.

If your daughter wanted to buy with her own money a baggy pair of jeans that was, in your eyes, particularly unflattering, would you let her? Do the jeans really matter, or are you concerned about what they say about *you* as a parent? Do you fear how you will look to your church or community if your child adopts the "grunge look"? But let's say you grit your teeth and acquiesce. Allowing your daughter to make this inconsequential decision actually gives you a foothold in her world. First, you've allowed her to express herself in a way that isn't threatening to anyone (except your comfort level), and, second, you've gained some of her trust. What does this add up to? Impartiality. Yes, one step closer to having heavenly wisdom. If her inner self hasn't changed, and she hasn't adopted a grunge attitude, there is nothing to be alarmed about.

The previous example is more likely to happen with girls who are close to or already fourteen. Sara's mom tells of a situation that shows another element of parental wisdom.

SARA'S MOM

ᴖ

Last year, when Sara was not even thirteen, she asked to have her ears pierced a second time above the holes she already had. I was against it. It seemed trendy to me, something she might regret later. Her dad had a fit. Even though he's outgoing and social, he's very conservative. His reply about the first holes had been, "If God wanted you to have holes in your ears, He would have put them there." I had to convince him then that the pierced ears were Sara's way of expressing her femininity.

But Sara's desire for two more holes seemed a result of peer pressure—a thought that scared both her father and me. Then as we talked with her about it and looked at her lifestyle, we realized that she wasn't running with a new group of friends, her grades were still high, and she still had a good sense of style in her clothes. The

added earrings would just be an expression of her indi-
viduality. Knowing that her clothes and her sense of
style are part of what makes Sara uniquely Sara, I felt
that second ear holes were a justifiable request.

Her dad took a little more convincing. But we both
came to realize that if we dug our heels in and denied
her request, we would be quenching her individuality,
something we had been trying to foster.

When her dad and I were finally in agreement, we
let her do it. I think our compromise with her really
helped us all recognize what is important in raising a
young woman and what isn't. Now if it had been a
nasal ring, that would have been a different story! Then
again, knowing Sara . . .

సా

This story is a great example of wisdom that is
peace-loving. What would fighting over this trivial
matter have gained? Nothing. Her parents wisely
recognized Sara's need to express herself in a manner that didn't harm anyone. They relaxed their own
ideals slightly to maintain peace with their daughter, without jeopardizing any of these ideals. Indeed,
if they had refused to let her get her ears done a second time, they may well have alienated her, and this
is not a time in her life when they should become her
adversaries.

You too can learn to let the little things go. Allow

her just enough freedom in decisions so that she feels they are truly her choices. What she wears (as long as it's relatively modest), how she wears her hair, her earrings, fingernail polish, etc., are just examples of her trying out different looks and characteristics. They help her to define who she is right now. Don't worry—she won't always want to have purple fingernails or earrings to her shoulders. These "accessories," like Sara's, are just an expression of who she feels she is right now.

DISTORTED BODY IMAGES

The flip side to your child's "trying on" different hats would be an attempt to have a body different from her genetic frame and body type. A fearsome thing is happening to young women in our culture. We call it the "Plague of Thinness." It's a plague because young women are literally starving themselves to death in search of the elusive perfect body. In 1995 the *American Journal of Psychiatry* reported that one woman in ten has symptoms of a serious eating disorder. Even more disturbing are studies that have shown that eating disorders can begin as early as ten or eleven years of age.

Just when your daughter starts to see changes in her body, she may become alarmed. For any number of reasons—fear, trauma, guilt, jealousy, perfectionism—she may turn to food as a way to control her increasingly out-of-control life. Anorexia (the person doesn't eat), bulimia (the person eats in binges and then vomits or uses laxatives to get rid of the food), and binge-eating (the person eats large amounts of food in a very short amount of time) are the clinical manifestations of a young woman struggling with her bodily self-image.

These are each extremely dangerous and serious illnesses because they become habitual and life-long patterns. The cause is usually rooted in a psychological factor and therefore needs to be treated not just as a medical crisis but as a psychological problem too.

If you are concerned that your daughter may have a tendency toward an eating disorder, look for these symptoms: severe restriction of calories, binge-eating, use of laxatives or forced vomiting, and avoidance of school or social functions to keep up with a strict exercise schedule.

Ellen struggles with her chunky frame, and her mom is very sensitive to Ellen's concerns.

ELLEN'S MOM

I know Ellen feels self-conscious about her heavy frame. I think that's why she felt so humiliated when her dad barged into the bathroom on her. She has become very cautious about what she eats, and though I think this is good and I encourage her to eat healthful food, I've been scared she could develop an eating disorder.

I've tried to use only positive language when I talk about her changing body, and I do believe she'll thin out some as she grows taller. But her body is not predisposed to thinness. All the women in my family are big-boned. We have wide hips, large bones, and stocky midsections. Ellen can't change the body type she's been given; yet she is struggling with the notion that she will be permanently "big."

I've shown her pictures of her grandparents and great-grandparents so she can see that she has inherited her body type. It helped a little. What has also helped, I think, is encouraging her to look at other people's bodies to see just how differently everyone is shaped. I've told her these differences are part of how God created us as individuals. She does understand that. I know she also draws caricatures of people who say what she feels are derogatory things to her. I think that helps her keep other people's opinions in perspective.

꒳

Another avenue Ellen's mom could try would be to talk about eating disorders. The notion that talking about them will put the idea in her daughter's head is unfounded. Telling her daughter about the consequences of eating disorders is not giving Ellen permission to try them but deterring Ellen from attempting any eating control.

If you fear your child has a tendency toward an eating disorder because she perceives herself as heavy, is having a difficult time with her changing body, is a perfectionist, or is acting out of control, talk to her. Describe the dangers of each disorder. You wouldn't just let her ride her bike in the street without warning her first of the risks and teaching her safety precautions. So warn her of the damaging, potentially life-threatening risks of these eating problems.

How can you support her during the times when she feels as if her body doesn't conform to the "ideal"? Your own example of healthy eating habits, not just what you eat, but *how* you eat, will teach her a positive attitude toward food.

Also reassure her about her "becoming" body. God isn't done growing her up yet—in mind, spirit, or body. In chapter 6 of *Just for Girls* we talk to your daughter about 2 Corinthians 1:21-22, which says, "He anointed us, set his seal of ownership on us, and put his Spirit in our hearts *as a deposit, guaranteeing what is to come*" (emphasis ours). As a child of His, your daughter has His promise, His guarantee, of continued growth in Him to become exactly who He wants her to be and look the way He wants her to look.

MENTORING

Another way to support your daughter during her years of development is to help her form a relationship with another older woman—her youth group leader, Sunday school teacher, previous baby-sitter, aunt, or older cousin. The thought of your child attaching herself to another woman can seem threatening, but the purpose is to give your daughter another person's perspective on her life issues. You and her father alone may not be able to meet all of her emotional needs. It's healthy for her to spend time with an older Christian woman who shares your values. It's sometimes easier for her to talk to someone besides her mother about her concerns, fears, or problems. Fostering and encouraging a semi-mentor relationship with a Christian woman shows your daughter you care enough about her feelings to offer another person with whom she can be comfortable. Discuss with this other woman your concerns about your daughter, but leave the rest of the relationship alone. The mentor shouldn't "report" anything to you about your daughter. Everything between them is in complete confidence unless your daughter is involved in dangerous behavior. Trust the relationship between the two of them to benefit all three of you.

DADDY'S LITTLE GIRL

A middle-aged woman we know vividly remembers the feelings she had about her puberty years and her father's response. When she was a child, her dad rubbed noses with her every night as he tucked her into bed. She loved hearing his footsteps climbing the creaking stairs each night for this ritual, giving her comfort and assurance as she settled to sleep every night.

Then one night when she was about eleven, he stopped. The stairs didn't creak at his approach, and she listened, waiting, until sleep claimed her perplexed mind. The next day she asked her mom why Dad hadn't come upstairs to rub noses with her. Her mom said, "You're grown up now, and it's not appropriate anymore." There was no more discussion. This young woman internally questioned, *Why?* Had she done something wrong? Did he not love her anymore? Why had her father rejected her?

Though now an adult with grown children of her own, she still feels sad and remembers the confusion she felt. It's only now that she sees he was uncomfortable with her advancement into womanhood. Instead of supporting her, he silently backed away.

Not enough can be said about the importance of a father's relationship with his daughter as she approaches puberty. A dad may feel confused about how to act as his daughter turns into a woman. Can he hug her, kiss her on the nose, put his arm around her?

Emphatically and absolutely, *YES!!!*

A father may subconsciously back off as his

daughter develops breasts and starts her period; after all, now she's a *woman*, right? Yes, her body is becoming womanly, but her emotional needs are greater than ever for a strong male figure who will treat her with respect and honor.

A dad has the ultimate responsibility to teach his daughter how she deserves to be treated by a man. He can open doors for her, listen to her words, encourage her talents, and compliment her on how she looks. A dad is modeling what his daughter should be seeking in a husband. Wow! A dad sets the stage for the kind of man with whom his daughter will want to spend the rest of her life.

Malachi 4:6 says, "He will turn the hearts of the fathers to their children, and the hearts of the children to their fathers." Dad's "heart"—his feelings, thoughts, and actions—need to turn toward his children, and particularly toward his daughter.

A young woman still needs hugs and kisses from her dad. She needs to feel his love, acceptance, and compassion. If a young pubescent woman doesn't receive a man's love and acceptance at home, she will look for it elsewhere. Studies have shown that an absent father, emotionally absent or physically absent, plays a major contributing role in a young woman's seeking out early sexual relationships. A young woman has a deep need to be loved and hugged; she needs to *belong* to someone. She needs to feel valued and important to someone. She needs to belong to her dad!

A dad can support his daughter with hugs, by looking her in the eye when he talks to her, by telling her he loves her, by going to her school events, by coaching sports teams she plays on, and by using upbeat, positive language. He can schedule time weekly to take her on a date, have a cup of tea with her at home, or even just drive her to school. *He needs to show her that, second to her mom, she is the most important woman in his life!*

SUPPORTING HER LIFE PLAN

In chapter 14 of *Just for Girls* we discuss with your daughter how to start a life plan—and let us reiterate that she doesn't need to make long-term choices about her career now! But it is good for her to think about different ideas that hold her interest. Why start now to think about possible life courses if she is only ten or twelve? Isn't that like putting the cart before the horse—giving her a job before she's even mature? Let us explain.

Her life plan simply gives her a purpose, something on which she can focus. It doesn't really matter what it is. It could be drawing, bicycle racing, hiking, piano playing, singing—whatever interests her now. It's good if she has several different appealing hobbies. Then she can combine them in some way.

What matters is that you support her and *believe in her ability* to follow her interest. Yes, it is likely to change in just a few short months or in a couple of years. But even if you have invested money in her to follow this early life plan, you have lost nothing. What you have gained is her trust in your assurance of support. She needs to explore different paths to find her niche. As the Lord grows her up, He will reveal more of her gifts and talents, which will give her a clearer view of where He is ultimately going to place her.

It's rather like climbing a mountain. There are a variety of paths leading to the summit. Some are relatively smooth; some are rocky; some require hand-over-hand climbing, but all lead upward. You have the ability to hold the guy ropes, supporting her climb and preventing a tragic fall. Your daughter may try a path, get stuck or discouraged, but then try a different route. She will eventually find the route that best requires her climbing gifts. Through all this, the point is that she is going upward, reaching for the top. The pinnacle is the adult plan God has for her, whether it is a job, ministry, marriage, or a combination of these.

MOM, WELCOME ANOTHER WOMAN
INTO YOUR HOME!

The support you offer your daughter for her physical, emotional, and spiritual needs is essential to her healthy development into a godly woman. You have a fragile young woman in your hands, a woman-child who needs special handling to prevent chipping or breaking. She is counting on you and her father to model Christian adulthood.

What a gift to be given the opportunity to raise a young woman in today's society! Scary, yes, because of the challenges women inherently face. But because of the spiritual wisdom available through Christ and the earthly knowledge about her body and mind, your daughter has an incredible advantage. With the tools we have given her and your guidance, she will grow into a woman of God with the potential to leave an indelible mark in people's lives.

Indeed, you are raising your daughter in a partnership with God. Philippians 1:5-6 says, "Because of your partnership in the gospel from the first day until now, being confident of this, that he who began a good work in you will carry it on to completion until the day of Christ Jesus." Your daughter is one of many good works God began in you, literally *in you*, and He promises to fulfill His end of the partnership in raising her. What a relief!

Your daughter has arrived at the intersection of childhood and womanhood. As she takes her first tenuous steps down the well-worn path, give her encouraging words, pat her on the back, and walk confidently with her.

You are her best resource and advocate as she scrambles along the rough path. You can point out the danger spots, grab her arm when she trips, and congratulate her when she reaches milestones. As she travels on her path, she will begin to shed her preadolescent self and in its place gather up her newfound womanhood, wrapping it confidently around herself.

The best equipment you can give your daughter is appreciation and respect for herself the way God made her. When she respects her body, sees it as God's gift, and has an enthusiastic desire to steward her womanly health for the Lord, few temptations can infiltrate her heart. You are equipping her now, at whatever age she is, to resist the world's fiery arrows by teaching her to honor her God-given body, mind, and soul and submit these to the Lord.

Action Points

🕮 Put together a personal hygiene kit for your daughter. You could decorate a pretty basket with ribbons or silk flowers and put in it deodorant, panty liners, "junior"-size tampons, an electric razor, deodorant soap, bubble bath, body lotion, facial cleanser, and sunscreen.

☞ Consider subscribing to a Christian teen periodical, such as Focus on the Family's *Brio* or Cook Communications Ministries' *The Rock.*

☞ For more information about preventing or treating eating disorders contact Eating Disorders Awareness and Prevention, P.O. Box 14469, Dept. P, Seattle, Washington 98114, phone: 1-800-969-6642. Or call National Association of Anorexia Nervosa and Associated Disorders at 1-847-831-3438.

BOOKS YOU MIGHT ENJOY

Anderson, Neil T. *The Bondage Breaker*. Harvest House, 1990.

Dobson, James. *Preparing for Adolescence*. Regal Books, 1989.

Dobson, James, and Gary L. Bauer. *Children at Risk*. Word Publishing, 1990.

Evans, Debra. *The Christian Woman's Guide to Sexuality*. Crossway Books, 1997.

Farrel, Pam. *Woman of Influence: Ten Traits of Those Who Want to Make a Difference*. InterVarsity Press, 1996.

Miller, Donna. *Growing Little Women: Capturing Teachable Moments with Your Daughter*. Moody Press, 1997.

Minirth, Frank, Paul Meier, Robert Hemfelt, and Sharon Sneed. *Love Hunger*. Thomas Nelson, 1990.

Newman, Deborah. *Then God Created Woman*. Focus on the Family, 1997.

Wolgemuth, Robert. *She Calls Me Daddy*. Focus on the Family, 1996.